First published 2001
exclusively for WHSmith by

Hodder & Stoughton Educational,
a division of Hodder Headline Ltd
338 Euston Road
London NW1 3BH

A CIP record for this book is available from the British Library.

Author: Graham Peacock

ISBN 0340 84604 6

Printed and bound by Graphycems, Spain

NOTE: The tests, questions and advice in this book are not reproductions of the official test materials sent to schools. The official testing process is supported by guidance and training for teachers in setting and marking tests and interpreting the results. The results achieved in the tests in this book may not be the same as are achieved in the official tests.

WH S

national TESTS practice papers

FOR THE YEAR **2002**

Science practice Papers

AGE
10-11
Key Stage 2

Contents

Page

Science at Key Stage 2

The first four of the tests in this book are aimed at children performing at Levels 3 to 5. These tests give children who are likely to achieve Level 3 the chance to answer a range of questions whilst, at the same time, offering a challenge to the more able pupils.

Performance at the different levels is summarised below.

Level 3	Level 4	Level 5
Children can describe differences and provide simple explanations. They can sort materials and living things and offer ideas about why materials are suitable for their purpose. When explaining how things work they link cause and effect, such as suggesting that the lack of light causes plants to become yellow. They also make generalisations about things they see, such as suggesting that it is difficult to see dim lights if they are near very bright lights.	Children can use more scientific terms such as the names of the organs of the body and those of flowering plants. They can use technical terms to describe processes such as evaporation and condensation. They can explain how differences are used to classify materials and living things systematically. They use their ideas about the way the physical world works when explaining how shadows are formed or the way that sound is heard through different materials.	Children can explain the factors behind why different organisms are found in different environments. They can describe the properties of metals and how they are distinct from other materials. They can identify why changes occur in materials and can suggest ways in which specific mixtures can be separated. They can use abstract ideas and models to explain physical phenomena such as the orbiting model of the earth to explain day and year length.

At Key Stage 2 it is possible for children to gain Level 6. This is unusual as few primary schools teach from the Key Stage 3 programme of study. However, some very able pupils will be able to tackle some of these questions.

At Level 6, pupils will be familiar with cell structure and the cause of variation between living things. They will recognise that materials are made up from particles and be able to recognise how new materials are formed in chemical reactions. They should be able to explain phenomena which involve a number of factors.

Setting the tests

There are five tests in this book. The last test is suitable only for very highly achieving pupils.

Give your child plenty of time to do each test – 35 minutes should be about right.

These tests can be a chance to confirm how well your child has done and how much he or she has learnt. Don't focus exclusively on what the child does not know.

There are 40 marks for each of the tests. Enter the mark in the box next to each question. Add the marks together at the end of each test and use them to assess your child's National Curriculum level on pages 38 and 46.

Reviewing progress

Perhaps the best use of these tests is for your child to do one every month or two from September onwards during Year 6. Discuss the tests and the answers at the back of the book. Talk about how the science relates to everyday life. During the year, your child should make some progress. It is this improvement rather than the absolute marks or your child's marks compared with other children that you should concentrate on.

Living in hot and cold places

1 The polar bear is adapted to live in cold, snowy places.

a Write TWO ways in which a polar bear is adapted to live in a cold, snowy place.

____

____

2

b Write TWO ways in which a rabbit is adapted to its habitat.

____

____

2

c These living things can be found in hot, dry countries.

Link each living thing to a label with a line.
The first has been done for you.

has spines instead of leaves to stop animals eating it
runs fast and has sharp teeth to kill prey
lives in a burrow during the hot part of the day
runs fast to avoid danger

3

TOTAL

7

Micro-organisms and change

2 Dean put yeast and water into four bottles.
He added sugar to bottle 1.
He added flour to bottle 2 .
He added salt to bottle 3.
He added nothing extra to bottle 4.

1. sugar 2. flour 3. salt 4. nothing added

a Which two bottles provided the best conditions for the yeast to grow?

____

2

b Why do you think two of the balloons began to swell?

____

____

1

c Yeast is a micro-organism.
Tick the pictures below where a micro-organism is involved.

1

Mouldy bread ☐ Making soap ☐ Making yoghurt ☐ Baking a cake ☐

TOTAL

4

3 Freda made bread.
She made a graph to show how long it took each loaf to rise.
Yeast is used to make bread rise.

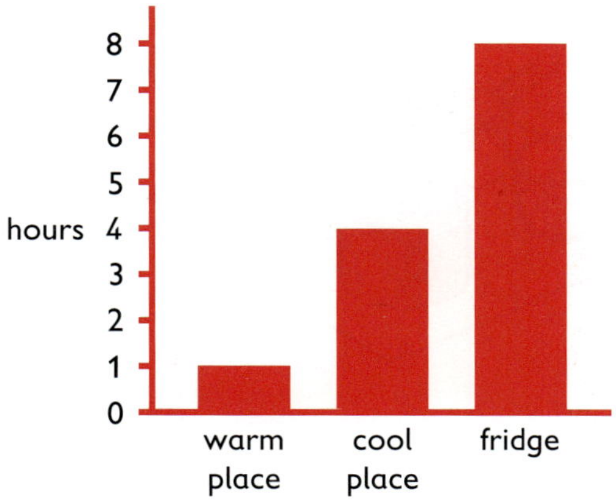

a Where did the bread rise most quickly?

____ 1

b Explain why you think it rose most quickly there.

____

____ 1

c Freda weighed the loaves before and after baking.
What do you think happened to the weight?

____

____ 1

d Give a reason for your answer to question c.

____

____ 1

e How do micro-organisms help in a garden compost heap?

____

____ 1

TOTAL 5

Comparing materials

4 These pan handles are made of different materials.

a Which handle will get hottest when the pans are used?

1

b Explain why.

1

c You would use an oven glove to pick up a hot handle.
Tick the box next to the material which would make the best oven glove.

aluminium foil ☐

thick cotton ☐

thin cotton ☐

1

d Explain your idea.

1

e Kate thinks that bubble wrap plastic would make a good oven glove.
Why would this not be a good material?

1

TOTAL

5

5 Mandy puts hot water into the bath.

a Why does the mirror become misty?

____

____

1

b The block of soap gets smaller as she uses it.
Why does this happen?

____

____

1

c Mandy records the temperature of her bath.
When the water cools, Mandy adds some more hot water.
She then continues with her bath.

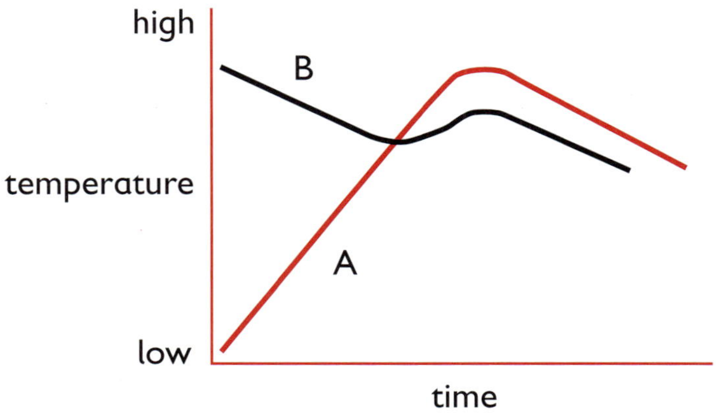

Which line graph shows the temperature in her bath?
Tick one box.

A ☐ **B** ☐

1

TOTAL

3

Weighing

6 Ann and Bill are weighing rocks.

Ann uses a spring balance to weigh a rock.
It measures weight in newtons.

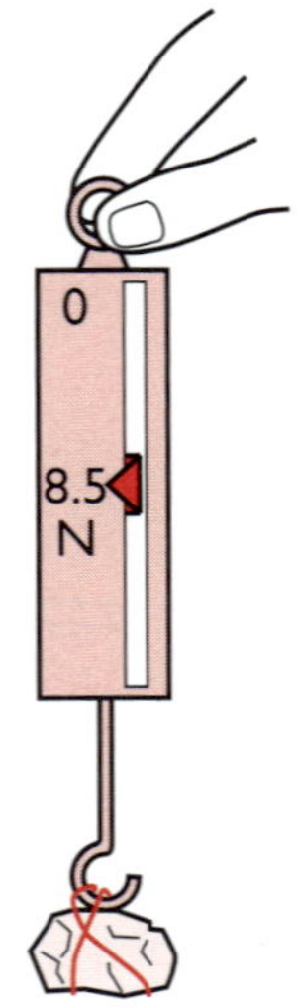

a What is the weight of the rock Ann is weighing?

____

1

b What force pulls the rock down?

____

1

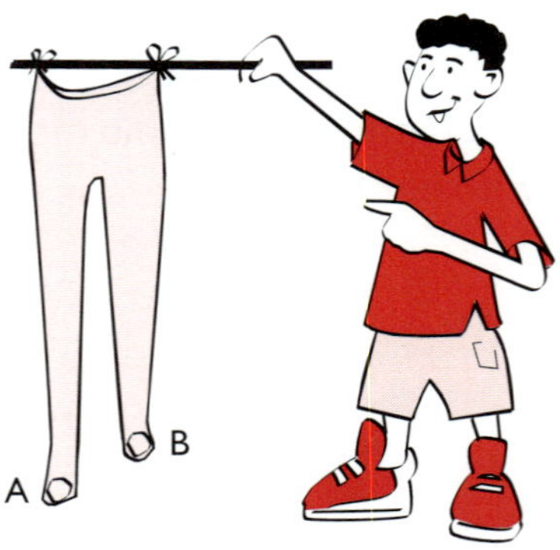

c Bill hangs a pair of old tights from a cane.
He puts a rock in each leg.
Tick the correct sentence.

Both rocks weigh the same ☐

The rock in A weighs more than the rock in B. ☐

The rock in B weighs more than the rock in A. ☐

1

d Explain your answer.
Use the word **gravity** in your explanation.

____

____

1

TOTAL

4

Mirrors

7 **a** Why are mirrors good reflectors?
Tick two boxes.

They are shiny ☐
They are hard ☐
They are in bedrooms ☐
They give out light ☐
They are smooth ☐

1

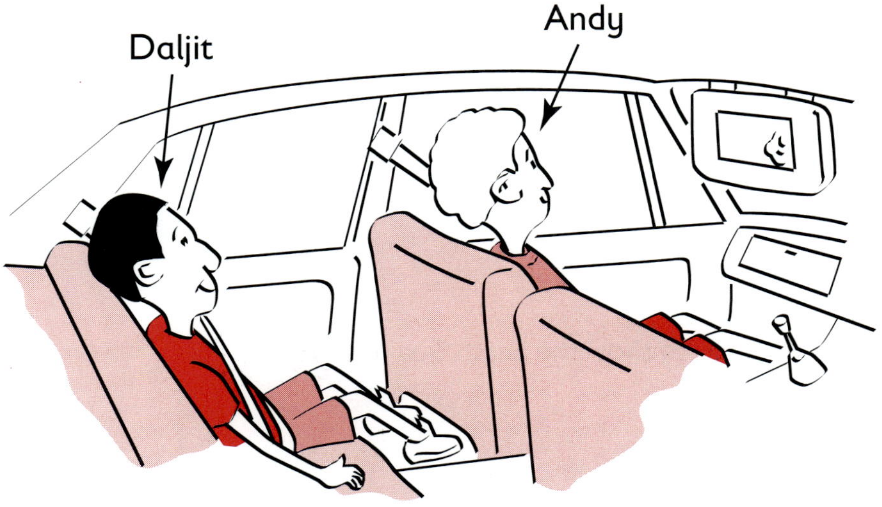

b Andy is looking in the car mirror.
He can see his friend Daljit.

Draw two arrows to show how he can see Daljit. 1

c Raj is using a periscope to see the match.
Draw arrows to show how he can see the ball. 1

TOTAL 3

The solar system

8 This is a diagram of the Sun, Moon and Earth.

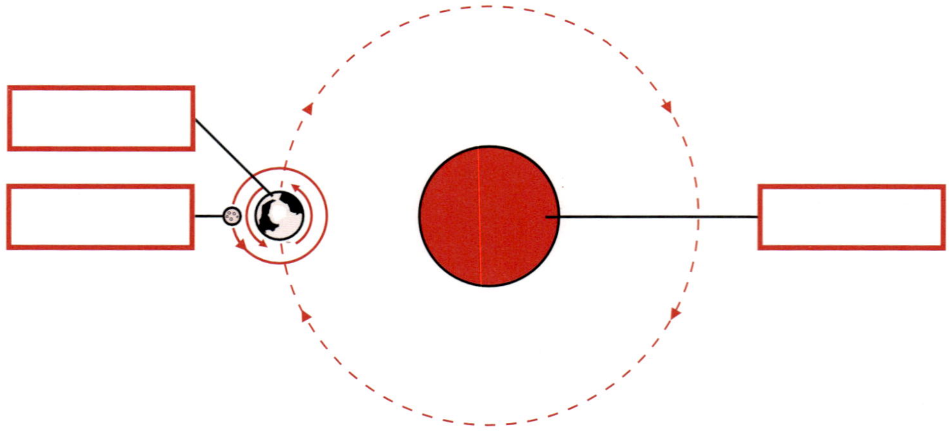

a Add labels to show the Earth, Sun and Moon. 1

b What shape is the Sun? 1

____

c Describe 2 ways in which the Earth moves. 2

i _______________

ii _______________

d Circle how long it takes for the Earth to orbit the Sun. 1

a day   a month

a year   a millennium

TOTAL 5

9 **a** What causes the Earth to have daytime and night?

____

____

1

b Complete this sentence.

When it is daytime in Britain it is .... in New Zealand.

1

c Why is sunrise in New York after sunrise in London?

____

____

1

d Tom has:

a beachball

a pea

a grape.

Which of these should he choose to show the relative size of the Earth, Moon and Sun?

Link them with a line.

1

Earth	**beachball**
Moon	**grape**
Sun	**pea**

TOTAL

4

Test 2

1 Identifying animals

a ____________________ **b** ______________________________

2

Write the name of the two animals above.
Use the key to help you.

1

c Does a dory have scales or feathers?

____

TOTAL

3

2 Plants

a Ann and Bill each planted a pea seed.
Ann's plant grew taller than Bill's plant.
Write two reasons which could explain this.

____

____

2

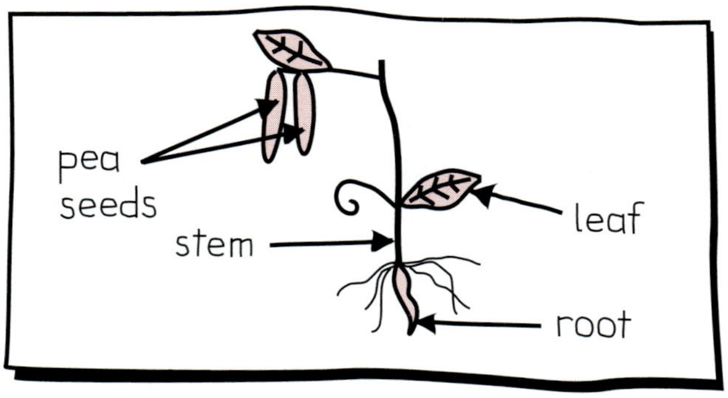

b What job do leaves do for a plant?

____

____

1

c What do the roots do for the plant?

____

____

1

d Ann tells Bill that pea plants do not have flowers.
Write what he should say to show she is wrong.

____

____

1

TOTAL

5

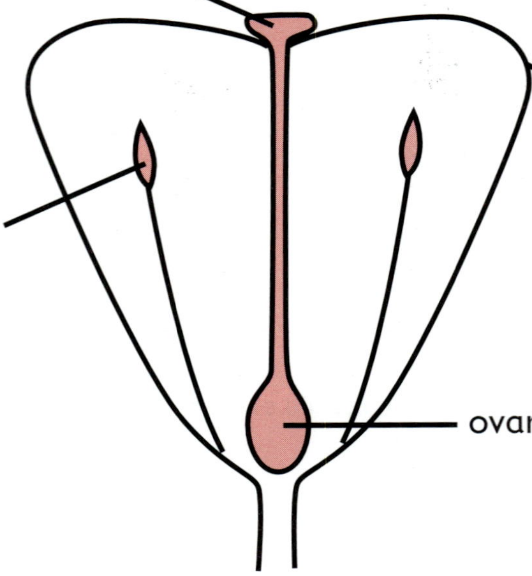

e Write the name of the correct part of the pea flower in the box.

The part of the plant where the seeds will form. [ ]

The male part of the plant which makes the pollen. [ ]

The female part of the plant which takes the pollen. [ ]

This attracts insects for pollination. [ ]

4

f Explain why it is important that all living things should reproduce.

____

____

1

TOTAL

5

3 Temperatures

a Ravi gently heated a block of chocolate in a pan.
Circle what happened to the chocolate.

It went brown | It melted | It set

1

b He mixed cornflakes into the chocolate.
He put the mixture in paper cases in the fridge. The mixture became solid.
Explain why it became solid.

____

____

1

c Ravi's dad mixed sugar and warm water in a pan.
Circle what happened to the sugar.

It melted | It dissolved | It evaporated

1

d He boiled the mixture to make toffee.
Circle what happened to some of the water.

It evaporated | It mixed in | It dissolved

1

TOTAL

4

4 **a** Link the labels to the correct temperature. One has been done for you.

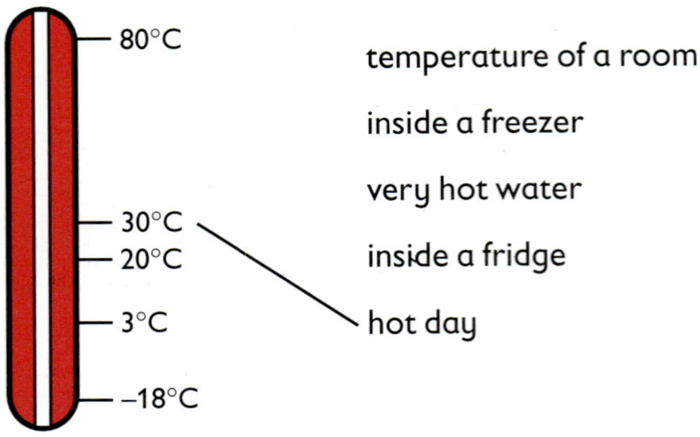

4

Lee put some ice in a tin.
He put a computer sensor into the ice and left it for two hours.
This graph showed what happened to the temperature.

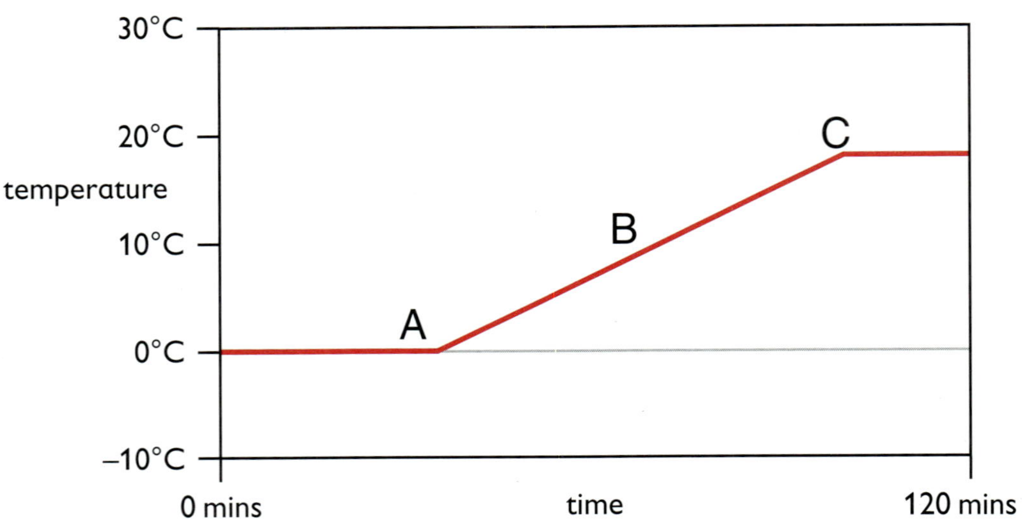

b The ice gradually melted.
Look at the graph.

At which point was there still ice in the water?

Tick one box.

A ☐
B ☐
C ☐

1

c What temperature do you think it was in the room where the experiment was carried out?

____

1

TOTAL

6

5 Magnets

The children tested the strength of magnets.
They counted the number of steel paperclips each magnet could lift in a line.

They recorded their results on a pictogram.
Each paperclip on the chart stands for a paperclip lifted by the magnet.

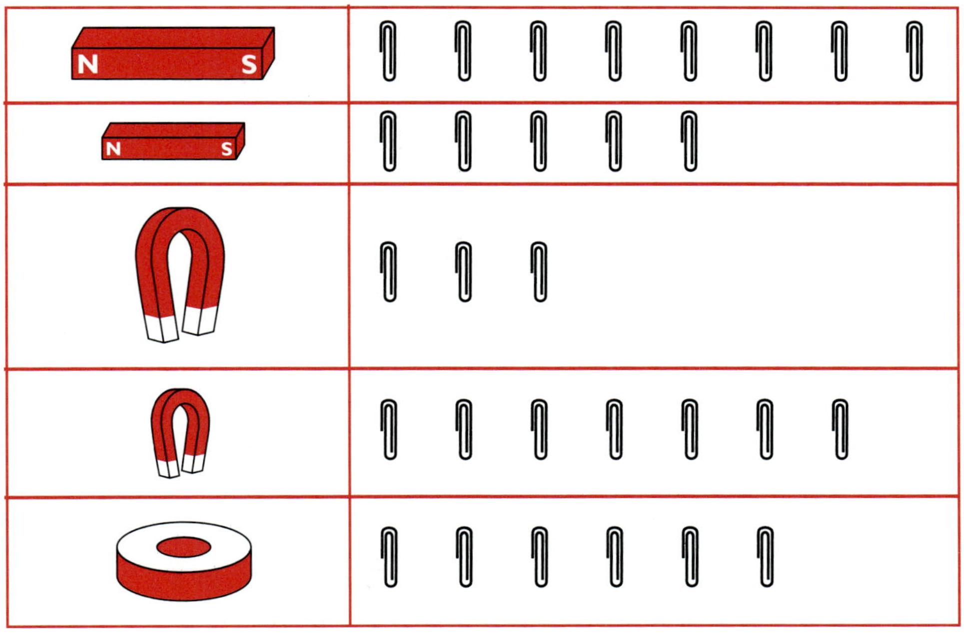

The children wrote about their results.

a Tick the sentences which are correct.

The large bar magnet held 8 clips. ☐

Large magnets are always stronger than small ones. ☐

The weakest magnet was a horse-shoe magnet. ☐

The large bar magnet held the most clips. ☐

All the horse-shoe magnets were weaker than all the bar magnets. ☐

3

b Jon played with two magnets.
He brought two south poles together.
What happened?

____

____

1

TOTAL

4

1

c Draw an arrow on the magnet to show the direction of the magnetic force on the paperclips.

2

d Would the children have got the same results with plastic paperclips? Explain your answer.

1

e Tracey finds that her magnets stick to the fridge door, but they will not stick to the wooden cupboard door.

What does this tell her about the material the fridge door is made from?

1

f Tracey is recycling cans. How could she tell the difference between aluminium and steel cans?

TOTAL

5

6 Shadows

The Sun's position in the morning is shown in the picture.

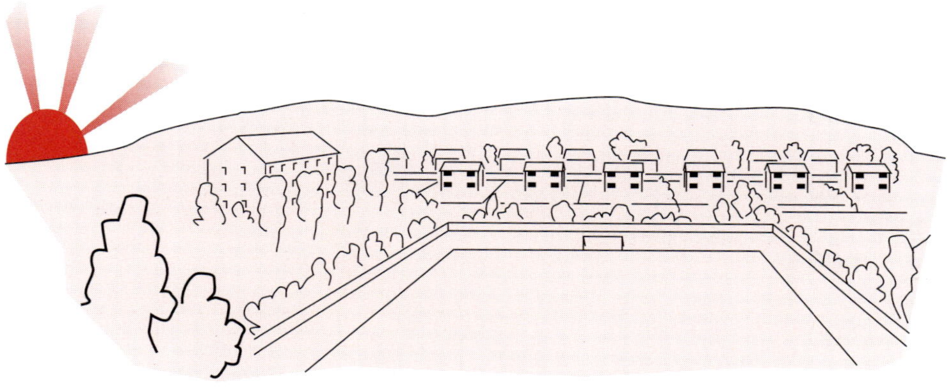

a Draw in and label the position of the Sun:

at noon

in late afternoon

2

b At what time of day will the shadows be shortest?

____

1

c Why are the shadows shortest at that time?

____

____

1

d Explain why the Sun seems to move across the sky.

____

____

1

TOTAL

5

Day length

7 This chart shows the approximate time of sunrise.
In May the Sun rises at 4.10 a.m.

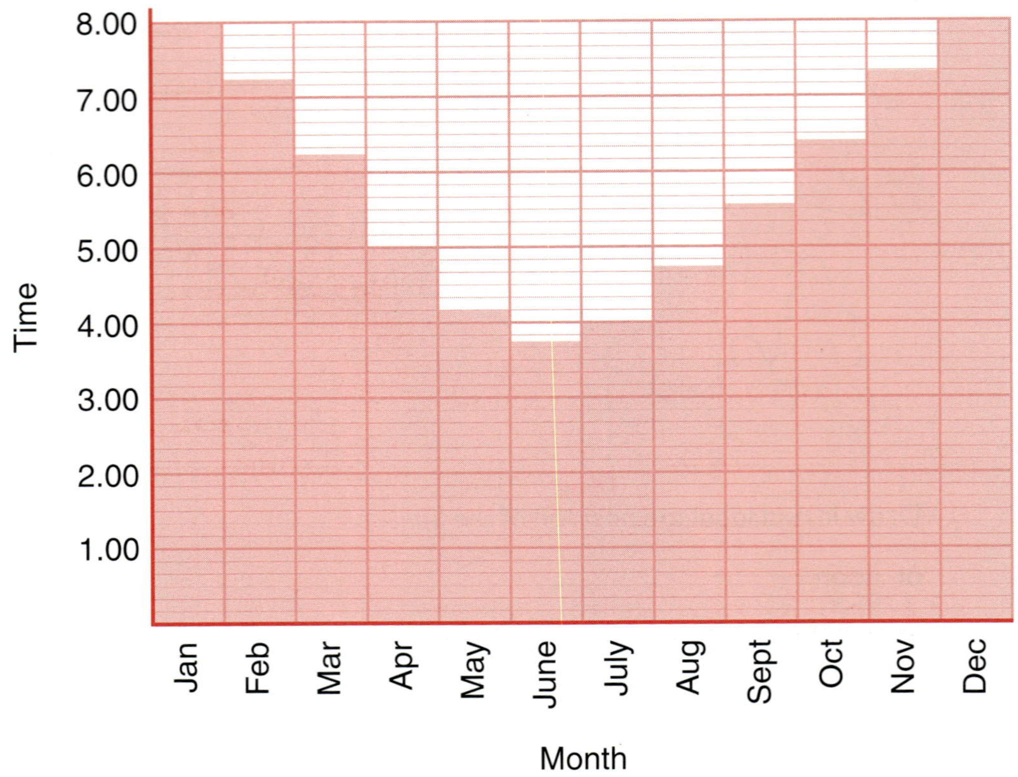

a What is the time of sunrise in February?

____

1

b What pattern do you notice about the time of sunrise from January to June?

____

1

c In which month do you think there is most daylight?

____

1

TOTAL

3

Living things

1 Class 2 wanted to find out which food slugs prefer.
They put 10 slugs into a box with 4 different foods.

After an hour they counted the number of slugs on each type of food.

They did this 3 times.

a Why did they do the test 3 times?

____

____

1

They recorded their results like this:

	lettuce	dry bread	potato	crisps
Test 1	5	1	4	0
Test 2	7	0	3	0
Test 3	5	2	3	0

b Which food did the slugs prefer?

____

1

c Did they like wet or dry food most ?

____

1

TOTAL

3

d Which other foods would slugs be most likely to eat? 2

Tick two boxes.

biscuits	cabbage	cornflakes	carrots

e Why do you think some gardeners do not like slugs? 1

____

____

f Slugs are eaten by birds such as thrushes. 1
Slugs eat plants.
Write a food chain for thrushes, slugs and plants.

.... → .... → ....

g Write a food chain which involves 1

tadpoles
pond weed
pike
stickleback

.... → .... → .... → ....

h Which FOUR things do ALL living things do? 4

- reproduce ☐
- run ☐
- get rid of waste ☐
- grow ☐
- see ☐
- fly ☐
- feed ☐
- talk ☐
- think ☐

TOTAL

9

Materials

2 **a** Tick the boxes next to the objects made of metal.

steel paperclip ☐

pencil ☐

brass pin ☐

iron nail ☐

plastic cup ☐

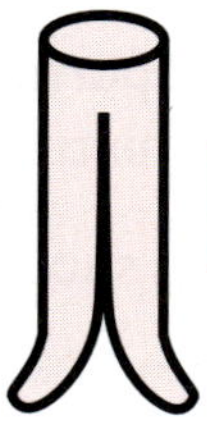
wooden peg ☐

1

b Connect the object to the right description with a line.

aluminium can	**does not conduct electricity**
iron nail	**non-magnetic metal**
plastic cup	**is magnetic**

3

TOTAL

4

Mixtures

3 **a** Jim and Jill have a mixture of salt and sand.
What can they do to separate the sand from the salt ?

Choose words from the list to complete the sentences.

dissolve	powder	water	sieve
filter	stir	sand	evaporate

They should add water to the mixture. The salt will .... but the sand will not.

To separate the sand and water, they should .... the mixture.

They should leave the mixture of salt and water in a dish. The water will

....

3

b How could each of these mixtures be separated?

Gravel and sand:

____

____

Iron nails and aluminium nails:

____

____

Matchsticks and small stones:

____

____

3

TOTAL

6

Circuits

4 Tansy tried to make a circuit with a bulb.

a Why will the circuit not work?

____

____

1

b Tick the materials which electricity could pass through to light the bulb.

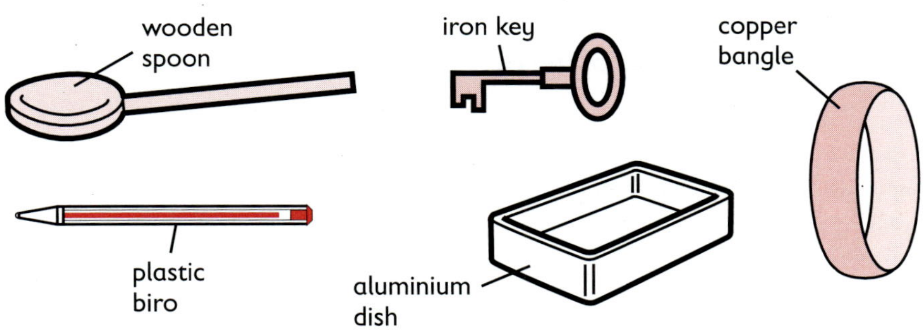

1

c Cloth and wood are examples of electrical insulators.
What is an electrical insulator unable to do?

____

____

2

TOTAL

4

5 Here are four circuit diagrams.

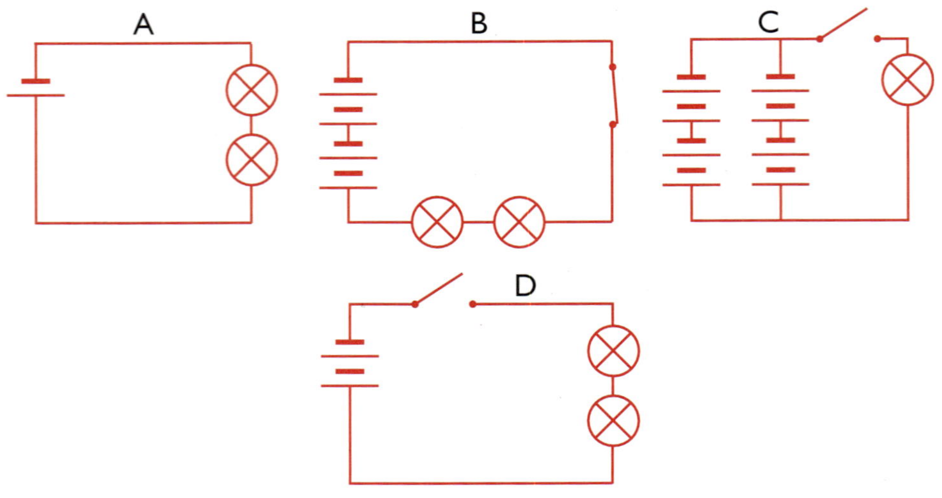

a Write the letter of the circuit which shows two bulbs and an open switch.

1

b Write the letter of the circuit which shows two bulbs and a closed switch.

1

c Write the letter of the circuit where there is no switch.

1

d Write the letters of two circuits in which the bulbs will be lit.

2

TOTAL

5

Light

6

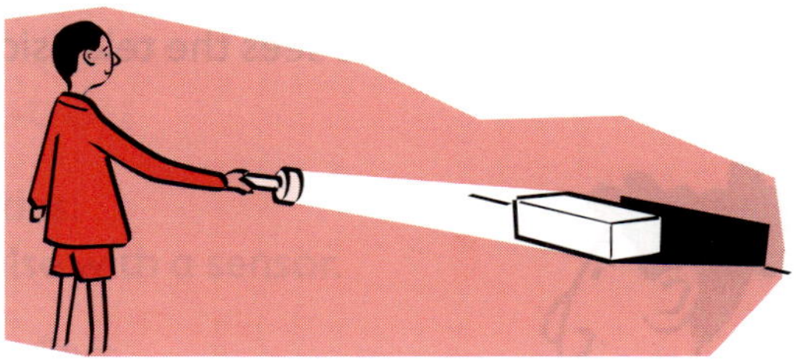

a Tom wrote these ideas about his shadow test.
Tick two boxes which show correct ideas.

The shadow is a reflection of the box. ☐

Two torches will make two shadows. ☐

The box makes a shadow because it is transparent. ☐

The box makes a shadow because it is opaque. ☐

2

b Tom recorded how the height of the shadow changed with the distance of the box from the torch.

Distance of box from torch	Height of shadow
50 cm	150 cm
100 cm	75 cm
150 cm	55 cm

Look at Tom's results.
Tick the correct answer.

The shadow got bigger as the torch moved away. ☐

The shadow got smaller as the torch moved away. ☐

Shadows don't change in size much. ☐

1

c This is a drawing of a cat's eye in a shady place.

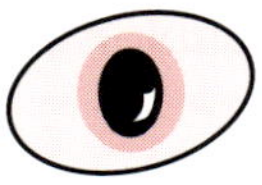

This is a drawing of the cat's eye in a sunny place.

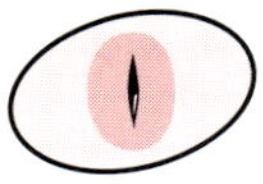

Explain why the two drawings are different.

____

2

TOTAL

5

5

2 **a** Join the labels to the correct bones of the skeleton.

These bones protect the brain.

These bones protect important nerves and keep you upright.

A hinge joint in the arm.

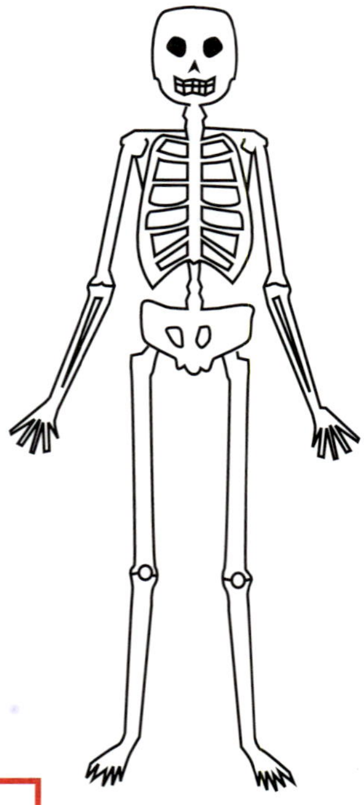

These bones protect the heart and lungs.

A ball and socket joint in the leg.

2

b Give two reasons why people need a skeleton.

____

____

TOTAL

7

Habitats

3

a Children in class 6 are studying habitats.

Write a habitat where each animal might be found.
The first has been done for you.
Write each habitat once.

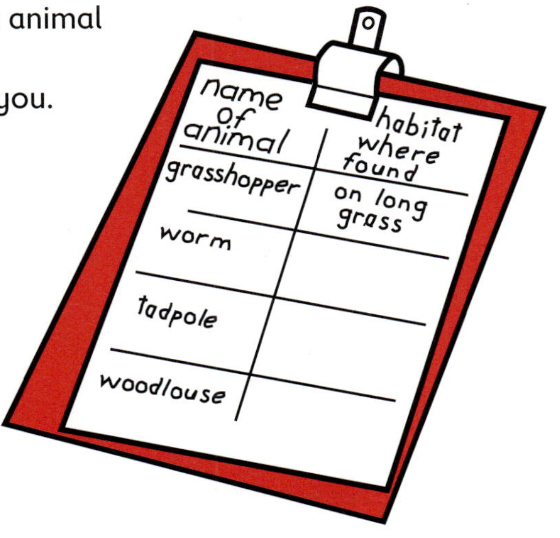

3

Class 6 counted the number of animals they saw in each habitat.

	on plants	on lawn	under a rotting log	on the wall
butterflies	4	1	0	1
ladybirds	2	0	0	0
slugs	2	0	8	0
spiders	0	0	5	2

b Which of the habitats had most animals?

____ 1

c Why were so few animals found on the lawn?

____

____ 2

TOTAL 6

4 Materials

a Give one reason why metal is a good material for making a trowel.

1

b Give one reason why plastic is a good material for making a hosepipe.

1

c Give one reason why the kneeling pad is made from foam.

1

d Tina's mum wants to separate the small stones from the soil. What is the easiest way to do this?

1

TOTAL

4

5 There is fizzy water in the glass.

a Write in the boxes to show which things are:

solid liquid gas

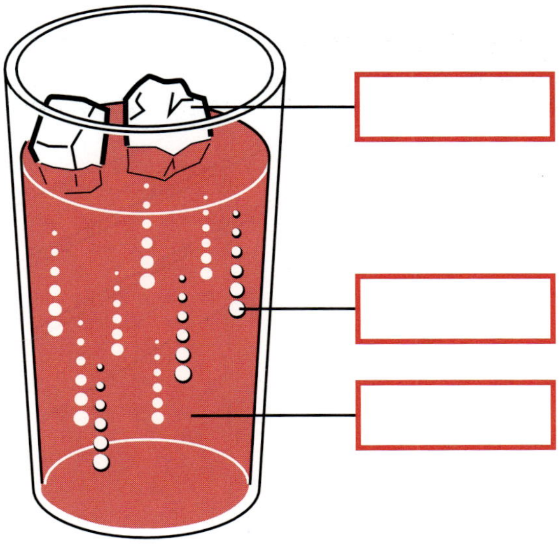

3

b Droplets form on the outside of the cold glass.
What process causes these to form?

____

1

c Where does the liquid come from to form these droplets?

____

____

1

d In hot weather, the level of water in a garden pond falls.
What process causes this to happen?

____

____

1

TOTAL

6

Forces

6 Jim tapes different-sized cards to identical toy cars.

a The cars will be let go at the same time.
Which car will stop first ?

1

b Explain why.

1

c Add an arrow to show the force of air resistance acting on this car.

1

TOTAL

3

Sound

7 Some children tested materials to see which one made the best ear muffs.

Janet put material into 2 cups and held the cups over her ears.
John turned the radio up until Janet could just hear it.
Fred did the same test as well.

Here is a table of their results.

material in the cups	volume when radio could just be heard	
	Janet	Fred
polystyrene	3	4
tissue paper	3	5
cloth	4	6
cotton wool	5	6

a Which material absorbed the least sound?

______________________________ 1

b Which material would be best to make sound-proof ear muffs?

______________________________ 1

c Which child had the best hearing?

______________________________ 1

TOTAL 3

The Moon and Sun

8 This is a drawing to show the Moon orbiting the Earth.

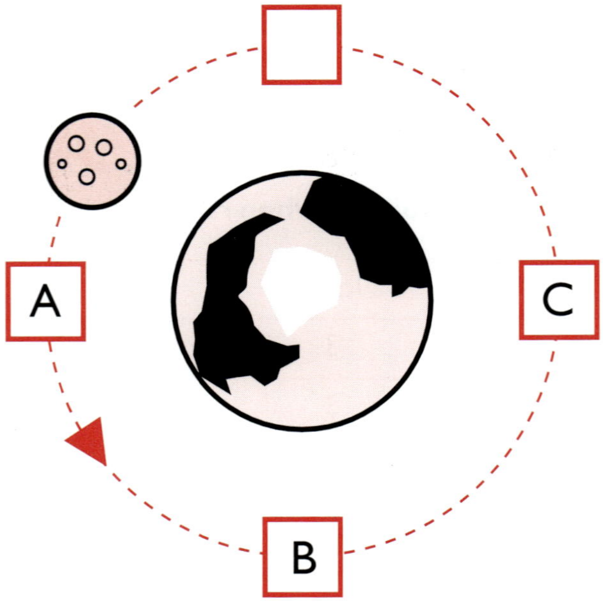

a How long does it take for the Moon to go from A to B?

____

1

b How long does it take for the Moon to go from A to C?

____

1

c The Moon does not give out any light of its own.
Describe how we can see the Moon.

____

____

1

d The Moon appears to be about the same size as the Sun in the sky.
Explain why you think the Sun and Moon appear to be the same size.

____

____

1

TOTAL

4

Answers

The words in brackets are not part of the answer you should expect from children.
All text in brackets is explanatory to help parents when discussing the answers with their children.

Question number	Answer	Mark
TEST 1		
1	**Living in hot and cold places**	
a	Having a white coat (for camouflage against the ice and snow) Having a thick coat (to insulate it) Having large paws (to stop it falling through snow and ice)	2
b	having large back legs (to run quickly) having a dull colour (for camouflage) having large (incisor) teeth (to eat vegetation) living in burrows (to hide from predators)	2
c	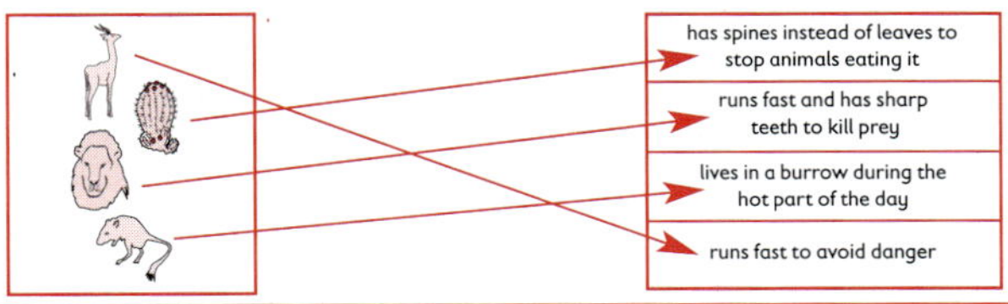	3
2	**Micro-organisms and change**	
a	Bottles 1 and 2 (this is because yeast 'eats' sugar and flour)	2
b	The balloons began to swell because the yeast gave off a gas.	1
c	mouldy bread ✓ (fungus) soap making (no micro organism involved) yoghurt ✓ (a bacterium turns milk to yoghurt thereby helping to stop it decaying) baking a cake (no micro organism – chemical raising agents such as baking powder)	1
3a	The bread in the warm place rose most quickly.	1
b	Because yeast works more rapidly in warm environments.	1
c	The weight of the loaf became less after baking.	1
d	This happened because water evaporated.	1
e	Micro-organisms help to decay plant waste to make the compost.	1
4	**Comparing materials**	
a	The metal handle will get hottest.	1
b	Metal conducts heat better than glass, wood or plastic.	1
c	Thick cotton will make the best oven glove.	1
d	Thick cotton is the best heat insulator.	1
e	The plastic would melt if it touched something hot.	1
5a	The mirror mists over when water vapour condenses on it (because the mirror is cold).	1
b	The soap gets rubbed off and dissolves.	1
c	Graph B	1
6	**Weighing rocks**	
a	The rock weighs 8.5 newtons. (the newton is the unit of measuring weight)	1
b	Gravity pulls the rock down.	1
c	The rock in A weighs more than the rock in B.	1
d	Rock A is pulled harder by gravity than rock B.	1
7	**Mirrors**	
a	They are shiny. They are smooth.	1
b		1
c	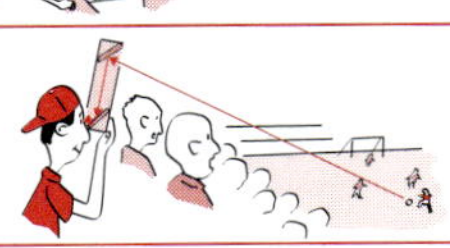	1
8	**The solar system**	
a	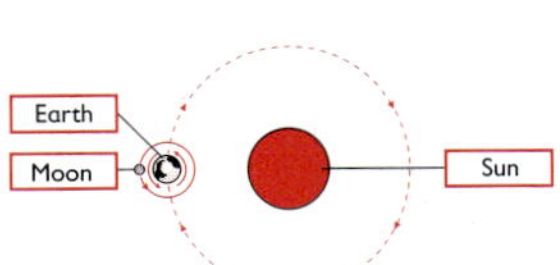	1

Answers

Question number	Answer	Mark
b	The Sun is spherical.	1
c	i The Earth turns on its axis.	2
	ii The Earth orbits the Sun.	
d	It takes a year to orbit the Sun.	1
9a	The Earth turns on its axis. (The part of the Earth which faces the Sun has day and the part which faces away from the Sun is in night-time)	1
b	When it is daytime in Britain it is **night** in New Zealand.	1
c	The time in New York is behind London because **the Earth turns** on its axis from east to west and New York comes into the Sun five hours after London.	1
d	Earth – pea Moon – grape Sun – beachball	1
TEST 2		
1	**Identifying animals**	
a and b	 a DORY b MONGOOSE	2
c	The dory has scales.	1
2	**Growing peas**	
a	Ann might have watered her plant more, kept it in a brighter place or planted it in better soil.	2
b	Leaves help the plant to make food.	1
c	Roots draw up water (and other nutrients) from the soil OR hold the plant in the soil.	1
d	Peas are seeds so the pea plant must have flowers to make seeds.	1
e	*The part of the plant where the seeds will form* **ovary** *The male part of the plant which makes the pollen* **stamen** *The female part of the plant which takes the pollen* **stigma** *This attracts insects for pollination* **petal**	4 *(1 mark each)*
f	Living things reproduce to make more of their own kind.	1
3	**Making sweets**	
a	It melted	1
b	The chocolate went solid because it cooled.	1
c	The sugar dissolved. (children frequently get confused between melting and dissolving. Melting would be incorrect in this instance)	1
d	Some of the water evaporated. (water does not need to boil to make it evaporate but heating speeds up the evaporation process)	1
4a	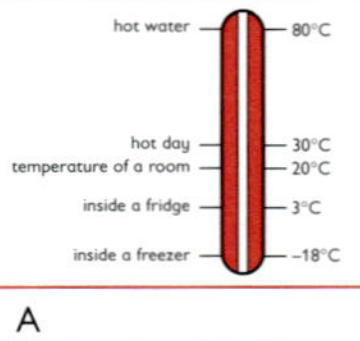	4
b	A	1
c	About 18°C (or any answer just below 20°C)	1
5	**Magnets**	
a	The large bar magnet held 8 clips. The weakest magnet was a horse shoe magnet. The large bar magnet held the most clips.	3
b	The two south poles repelled each other.	1
c	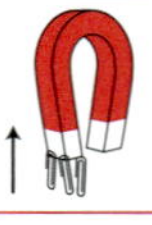	1
d	No. Plastic is not attracted to magnets. (phrases such as 'plastic is not magnetic' are also acceptable)	2
e	The fridge is made from either steel or iron. *or* The fridge door is made from a magnetic material.	1
f	Test them with a magnet. Aluminium is not attracted to magnets.	1
6	**Shadows**	
a	 noon late afternoon	2
b	The shadows will be shortest at noon.	1
c	The shadows are shortest because the Sun is at its highest in the sky at noon.	1
d	The Sun appears to move across the sky because of the way the Earth turns on its axis.	1

Question number	Answer	Mark
7	**Day length**	
a	7.15 a.m.	1
b	The Sun gets earlier from January to June.	1
c	There is most daylight in June (because the Sun rises earlier)	1
TEST 3		
1	**Living things**	
a	They did the test three times to check their results.	1
b	Lettuce	1
c	The slugs liked wet food best.	1
d	Carrots and cabbage (as these are most like the favourite ones above)	2
e	They eat the plants the gardeners are trying to grow.	1
f	plants → slugs → thrushes	1
g	pond weed → tadpoles → stickleback → pike	1
h	Reproduce; get rid of waste; grow; feed.	4
2	**Materials**	
a	steel paperclip, brass pin, iron nail	1
b	Aluminium can is non-magnetic metal. Iron nail is magnetic. Plastic cup does not conduct electricity.	3
3	**Mixtures**	
a	They should add water to the mixture. The salt will **dissolve** but the sand will not. To separate the sand and water, they should **filter** the mixture. They should leave the mixture of salt and water in a dish. The water will **evaporate**.	3
b	Gravel and sand: sieve (let the sand fall through a sieve) Iron nails and aluminium nails: magnet (the iron will be attracted to the magnet) matchsticks and stones : float (the sticks will float and the stones will sink)	3
4	**Circuits**	
a	The two batteries are connected the wrong way round. (There are two positive terminals connected together. A positive should be connected to a negative in series.)	1
b	Electricity will pass through the iron key, the copper bangle and the aluminium dish (all these are metals).	1
c	Electrical insulators do not allow electricity to pass through.	2
5		
a	D	1
b	B	1
c	A	1
d	A and B	2
6	**Light**	
a	Two torches will make two shadows. The box makes a shadow because it is opaque. (Children often get reflections and shadows confused. Transparent things do not make a good shadow as the light passes through them.)	2
b	The shadow got smaller as the torch moved away.	1
c	The cat's pupil is larger in the shady place to let more light in.	2
7		
a	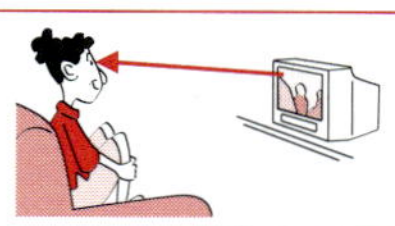	1
b	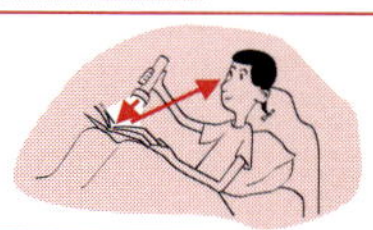	1
c	Sun burning coal	2
TEST 4		
1	**The human body**	
a	(table below)	3

	Arun's pulse rate per minute	
	Doing activity	After five minutes' rest
Playing cards	85	80
Walking on the flat	95	80
Walking up stairs	between 100 and 110	80
Running up stairs	115	80

Question number	Answer	Mark
b	His heart pumped more blood round the body *or* his body needed more oxygen so the blood needed to go faster.	1
c	It pumps blood around the body (to supply more food and oxygen to his muscles).	1

Answers

Question number	Answer	Mark
d	eating less fatty food exercising regularly	2
2a	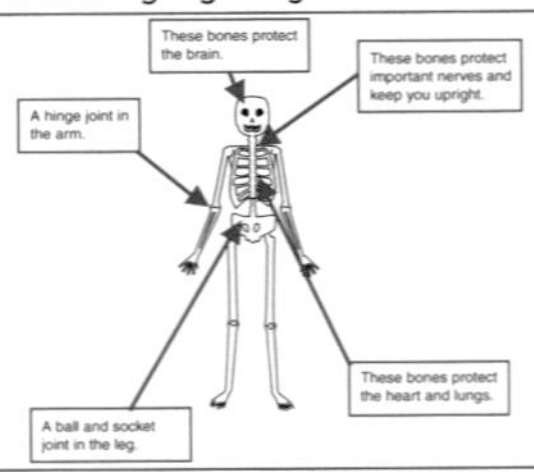	5
b	to support their bodies to protect organs	2
3	**Habitats**	
a	worm … soil tadpole … pond woodlouse … log	3
b	Under a rotting log (because the habitat provided shelter and food)	1
c	The grass is short and there is no food and shelter for small animals.	2
4	**Materials**	
a	Metal is good for making a trowel because it is strong.	1
b	Plastic is good for a hosepipe because it is bendy and waterproof.	1
c	The kneeling pad is made from foam because it is soft.	1
d	She should use a sieve.	1
5a	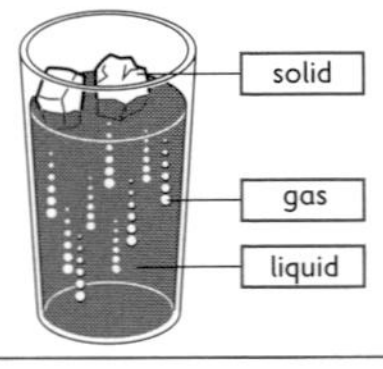	3
b	Condensation	1
c	The liquid comes from the air (water vapour in the air)	1
d	Evaporation causes the water level to drop.	1
6	**Forces**	
a	The car with the biggest air brake / piece of card will stop first (A).	1
b	It will have the most air resistance slowing it down.	1
c	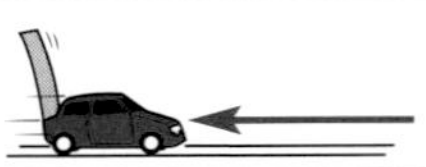	1
7	**Sound**	
a	polystyrene	1
b	cotton wool (the radio had to be turned up highest to hear through this material)	1
c	Janet (she could hear at lowest volumes)	1
8	**The Moon and Sun**	
a	It takes one week for the Moon to go from A to B (quarter orbit).	1
b	It takes two weeks for the Moon to go from A to C.	1
c	The Moon reflects the Sun's light.	1
d	The Moon is much closer to us than the Sun.	1

National Curriculum Levels

Each test is worth 40 marks. For Tests 1 to 4, the scores achieved indicate the following National Curriculum level.

Mark	0–17	18–25	26–33	34–40
Level	Level 2	Level 3	Level 4	Level 5

If your child scores highly on these tests, he or she could try the Level 6 Extension Paper on the next page.

If your child needs more practice in any Science topics, use the WHSmith Key Stage 2 Science Revision Guide.

New substances

1 Candle wax is a compound of hydrogen, carbon and oxygen.

a Name two substances which are formed when wax burns.

____

____ 2

b Describe what happens when a candle burns.

Use these words in your writing:

evaporate   solidity   melt   burn

____

____

____

____ 4

c Rust is a compound of substances.

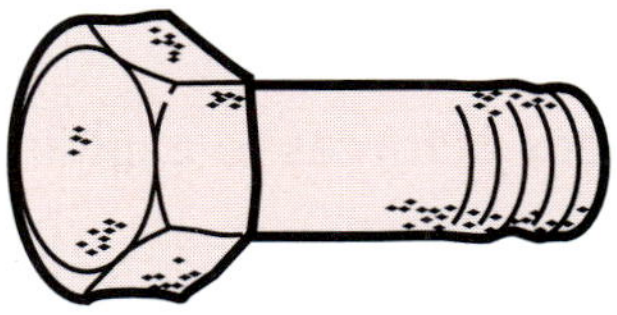

What are substances are needed to form rust?

____

____ 2

TOTAL 8

Changing speed

2 These drawings show the forces of air resistance and the forward push of a hovercraft.

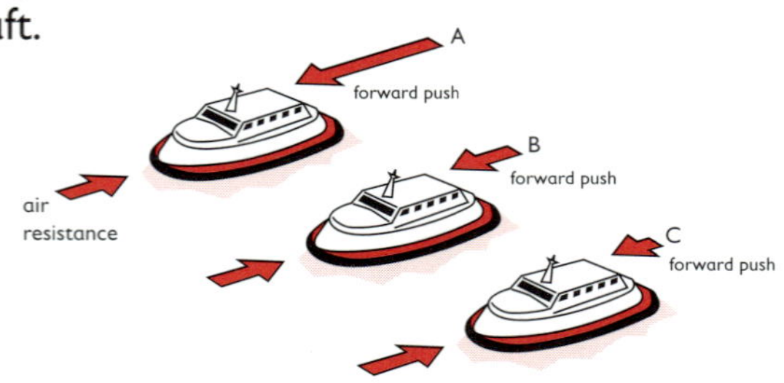

a Which drawing shows the hovercraft going faster? ☐ 1

b Which drawing shows the hovercraft slowing down? ☐ 1

c Which drawing shows the hovercraft moving at a constant speed? ☐ 1

d Explain your answer to question c. 1

____

____

This line graph shows the speed of a car over 30 seconds.

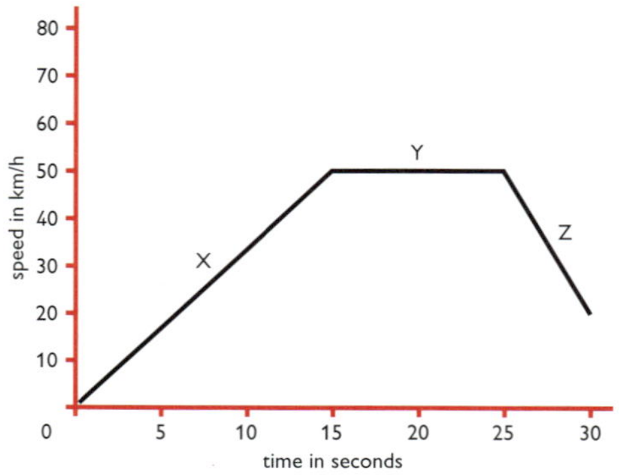

e What is happening to the speed of the car at X? 1

____

____

f Use the ideas of forces to explain what is happening at point Y. 1

____

____

g Use the ideas of forces to explain what is happening at point Z. 1

____

____

TOTAL 7

Plant and animal cells

3 Tim looked at a plant cell through a microscope.
He saw the vacuole, cell wall, chloroplasts and nucleus.

a Label this drawing of a plant cell. 4

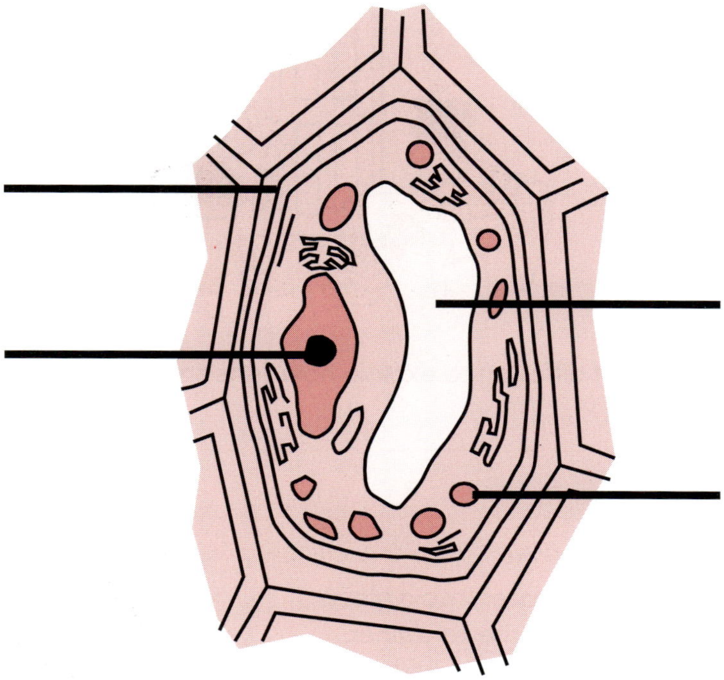

b Which part of the plant cell helps carry out photosynthesis? 1

____

c Which two compounds do plants use in photosynthesis? 2

____

____

d Tim looked at an animal cell through a microscope.
He noticed differences between plant and animal cells.

Write down two differences between plant and animal cells. 2

____

____

TOTAL 9

Particles

4 **a** Jane is sitting in a still room.
Hazel puts some perfume on her skin.
A few seconds later Jane smells the perfume.

Use the idea of diffusion to explain how Jane smells the perfume.

____

____

1

b Kate pours liquid water into a glass.
It takes the shape of the container.
She fills another container with ice cubes.
These stay in their original shape.

Use the idea of particles to explain the differences between ice and liquid water.

____

____

1

c Water evaporates more quickly when it is heated.
Explain how heating affects water particles, leading to more rapid evaporation.

____

____

1

TOTAL

3

The solar system

5 Looking up into the night sky, Pam saw the planets Venus and Jupiter. She knew that planets are not light sources.

a Explain how Pam could see these planets.

____ 1

____

b Venus looked much brighter than Jupiter.
Pam knew that Jupiter was much larger than Venus.
Explain why Venus is brighter than Jupiter.

____ 1

____

c One evening Pam saw shooting stars.
Explain how these are formed.

____ 1

____

d What is the force which causes the Earth to stay in orbit around the Sun?

____ 1

e List the five planets in the solar system which are nearest to the Sun.
Start with Mercury.

Mercury 1

____

____

____

____

f Explain why the Moon rises in the east and sets in the west.

____ 1

____

TOTAL 6

Circuits

6 This circuit diagram shows three identical bulbs.

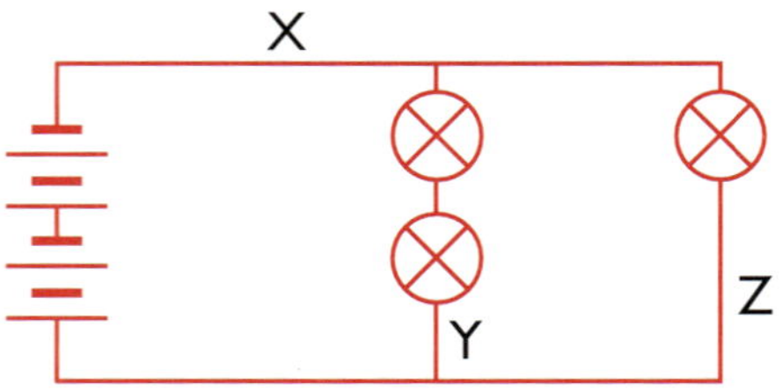

Which of these statements are true about this circuit?

a Tick the true statements.

The current at Z is greater than at Y. ☐

The current at Z is equal to Y. ☐

The current at X is the same as Y plus Z. ☐

The current at X is equal to the current at Y. ☐

The current at X is equal to the current at Z. ☐

2

b These two circuits have the same number of batteries and a different number of bulbs.

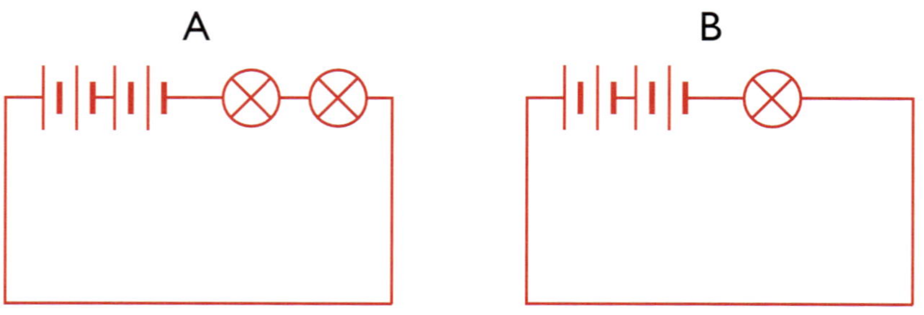

Use the idea of electrical resistance to explain why the bulb in circuit B is brighter than the two bulbs in circuit A.

____

____

1

TOTAL

3

Forces and motion

7 These two men are travelling through deep snow. Man A is wearing ordinary shoes. Man B is wearing skis.

a Explain why the small man A sinks deeper into the snow than the heavier man B.

____

____

1

b Which of these skiers is likely to travel faster?
Explain your idea.

____

____

1

c The faster skier finishes a 200 m downhill race in 20 seconds.
What is her average speed in metres per second?

____

1

d The slower skier finishes the same race in 25 seconds.
What is her average speed in metres per second?

____

1

TOTAL

4

Answers

Test 5

Question number	Answer	Mark
1	**New substances**	
a	carbon dioxide water	2
b	Answers will vary, but as an example: The candle wax melts. It evaporates off the candle wick and burns. Wax that dribbles down the side solidifies when it cools enough.	4
c	iron oxygen	2
2	**Changing speed**	
a	A	1
b	C	1
c	B	1
d	In drawing B the forces are equal and the craft is neither slowing down nor speeding up.	1
e	The car is getting faster / accelerating.	1
f	It is travelling at a constant speed and the forces are equal.	1
g	It is slowing because the forces of air resistance and friction are greater than the push from the engine.	1
3	**Plant and animals cells**	
a	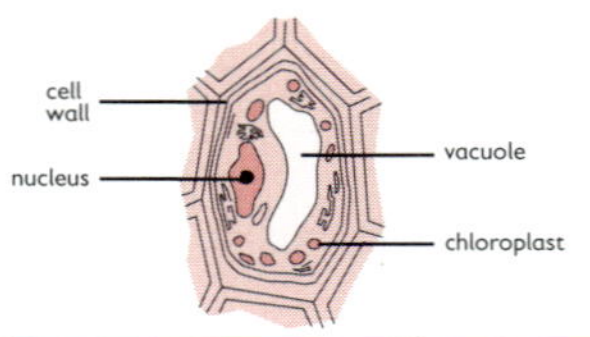	4
b	chloroplast	1
c	carbon dioxide and water.	2
d	Animal cells do not have the following structures, which are present in plant cells. Chloroplast Vacuole Cell wall	2
4	**Particles**	
a	The liquid perfume evaporates and turns into a gas which diffuses through the air.	1
b	In solids the particles are held firmly together and cannot move. In a liquid the particles can move past each other.	1
c	Heating gives particles more energy so that they break the bonds with the other molecules in the liquid.	1
5	**The solar system**	
a	Planets reflect light from the Sun.	1
b	Venus is brighter because it is a lighter colour and it is closer to the Earth and to the Sun.	1
c	Particles of dust burn up in the Earth's atmosphere as they enter the atmosphere at high speed. This speed results in very high levels of friction.	1
d	Gravity	1
e	Mercury Venus Earth Mars Jupiter	1
f	This is caused by the Earth turning on its axis.	1
6	**Circuits**	
a	It is true that: • the current at Z is greater than at Y • the current at X is the same as Y + Z.	2
b	In circuit A, the resistance of the two bulbs is combined, resulting in greater resistance. This means that less electrical current will flow in A.	1
7	**Forces and Motion**	
	a Man B is spreading out his weight using skis. (This means there is less pressure on the snow so he does not sink into it.)	1
	b The crouched man will travel more quickly as he is offering less air resistance.	1
	c 10 metres per second	1
	d 8 metres per second	1

National Curriculum Levels

For Test 5, the marks indicate the following levels.

Mark	0–20	21–30	31–40
Level	Level 4	Level 5	Level 6